piano · vocal · guitar

themart

glorifyedifytestify

2
Standing on the Promises

13
You Are Holy

19
Pass Me Not

27
Settle on My Soul

36
I Could Sing of Your Love Forever

44
Great Is the Lord

53
Healer of My Heart

62
Redeemed

68
So High

80
Be Thou My Vision

85
Jesus, I Am Resting

93
In Christ Alone

101
Gentle Shepherd/Leaning on the Everlasting Arms

108
Lord Most High

115
My Jesus, I Love Thee

ISBN 0-634-05155-5

HAL•LEONARD®
CORPORATION
7777 W. BLUEMOUND RD. P.O. BOX 13819 MILWAUKEE, WI 53213

Visit Hal Leonard Online at
www.halleonard.com

STANDING ON THE PROMISES

Words and Music by DAVE CLARK
and BILL BAUMGART

Moderately fast

Male vocal sung as written.

YOU ARE HOLY

Words and Music by GRANT CUNNINGHAM,
MATT HUESMANN and CHRISTOPHER DAVIS

Slowly

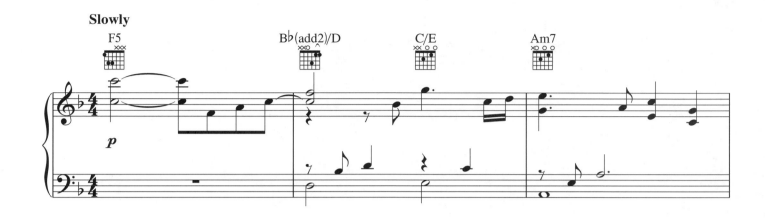

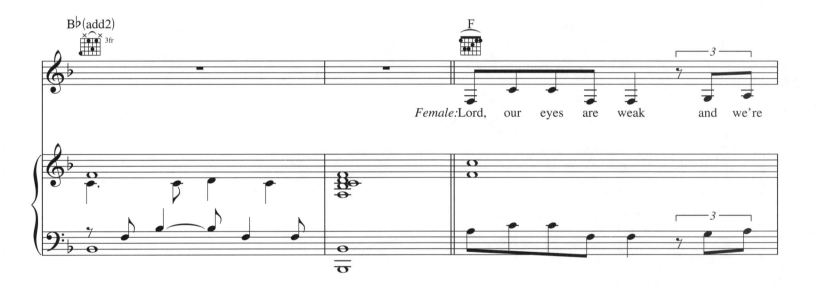

Female: Lord, our eyes are weak and we're

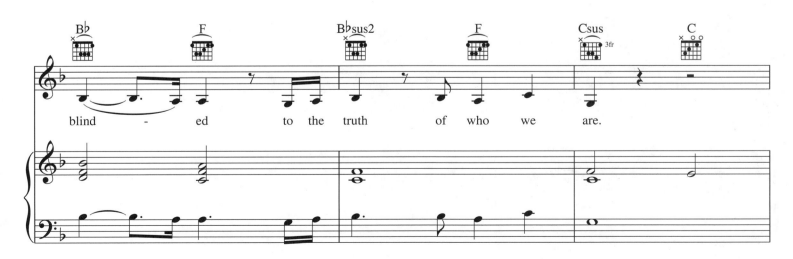

blind - ed to the truth of who we are.

Ev-'ry time we look, we're re-mind—ed of the things that stain our

heart, *All:* why You are ho—ly, ho — ly. ___

Ho — ly are You, Lord, and You are wor—thy

wor — thy. ___ Wor—thy are You, ___ Lord. ___

* Male vocal sung as written.

PASS ME NOT

Traditional
Arranged by THE MARTINS
and ROBERT WHITE JOHNSON

All: Ooh. _____

Male: Pass me ___ not, O, gen - tle Sav - ior.

* *Male vocal written one octave higher than sung.*

C
G
G9
9fr
hear my hum - ble cry.
C
C9
F
C
Am
While on oth - ers Thou art call - ing,
F6
C/G
Dm7/G
C
C9
3
do not pass me by.
3
F6
C/G
Dm7/G
C
G9
9fr
Do not pass me by.
3
8vb

SETTLE ON MY SOUL

Words and Music by
JAKE HESS JR.

Male vocal sung as written.

Original key: B major. This edition has been transposed down one half-step to be more playable.

Let the veil fall from my face; __ re-veal Your mys - ter - ies. __

Let me feel Your ____ em - brace. __

Warm my un - be - lief. ____ Set - tle on my

soul, sweet __ Je - sus. Set - tle down on ____ me. ____

I COULD SING OF YOUR LOVE FOREVER

Words and Music by
MARTIN SMITH

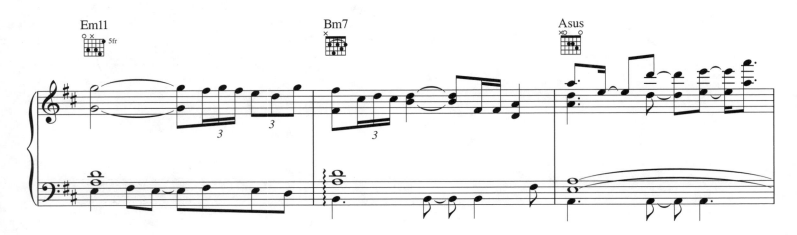

1. *Male*:
2. *Female*: O - ver the moun - tains and ___ the sea

* Male vocals written one octave higher than sung.

GREAT IS THE LORD

Words and Music by MICHAEL W. SMITH
and DEBORAH D. SMITH

Martins: Great is the Lord; He is ho-ly and just. By His pow-er we trust in His love.

* Male vocal sung as written.

HEALER OF MY HEART

Words and Music by ROBERT WHITE JOHNSON
and JAMES ROBINSON

Moderately slow, freely

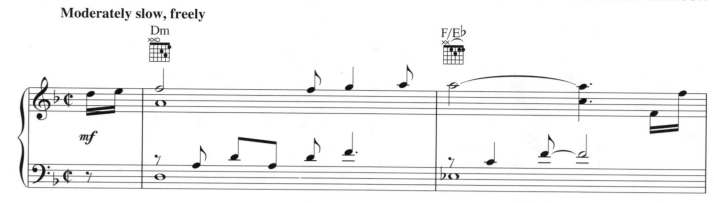

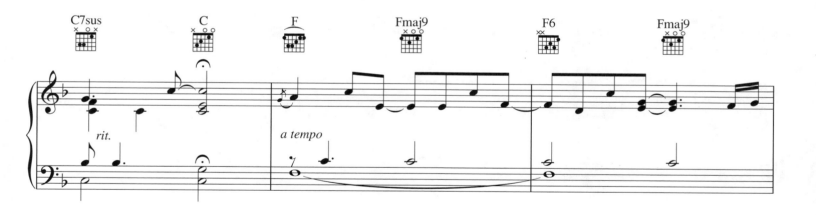

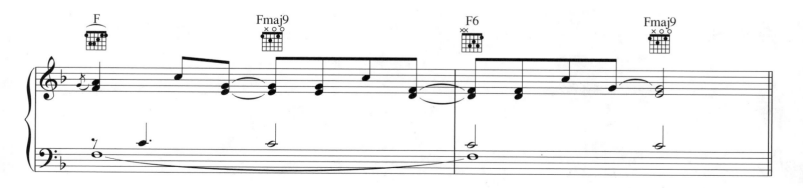

* Male lead vocal written one octave higher than sung.

* *Male harmony sung as written.*

REDEEMED

Traditional
Arranged by THE MARTINS
and ROBERT WHITE JOHNSON

Male vocal written one octave higher than sung.

SO HIGH

Traditional
Arranged by THE MARTINS
and ROBERT WHITE JOHNSON

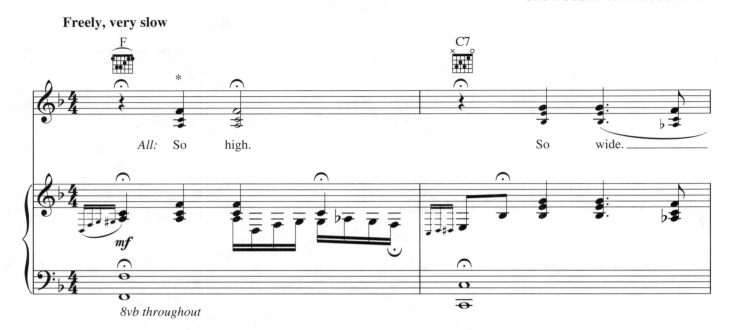

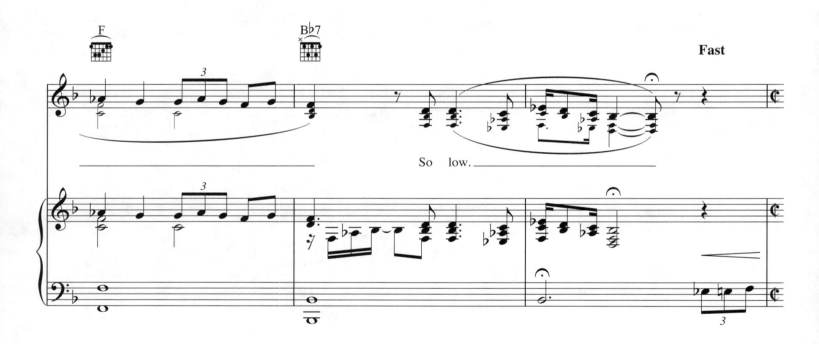

* Male vocal sung as written.

So high you can't get o - ver it.

So wide you can't get a - round__ it.__

So__ low you can't get un - der it. You

just stayed there all day.

loco-- ┘   *8vb throughout*

All: I went down to the val - ley; I

did not go to stay, but

my soul got so hap - py I

streets are _____ pur - est _____ gold. _____

8vb throughout

Men: It's so high. _____
_____ It's so _____ high. _____
(High you can't get o - ver it.)

It's _____ so

It's so _____ wide. _____

Male harmony written one octave higher than sung.

loco throughout

BE THOU MY VISION

Traditional
Arranged by THE MARTINS
and ROBERT WHITE JOHNSON

Female: Be Thou My ____
Male & Female: Be Thou My ____

* Male vocal written one octave higher than sung.

vi - sion, O ___ Ru - ler of all. ___

JESUS, I AM RESTING

Traditional
Arranged by BUDDY GREENE

Moderately

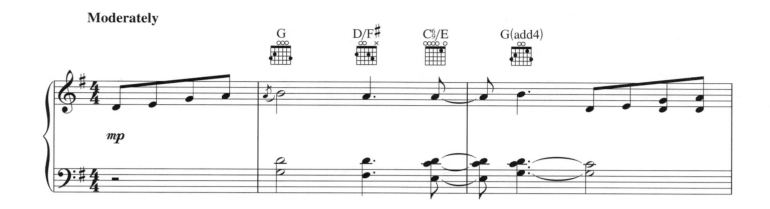

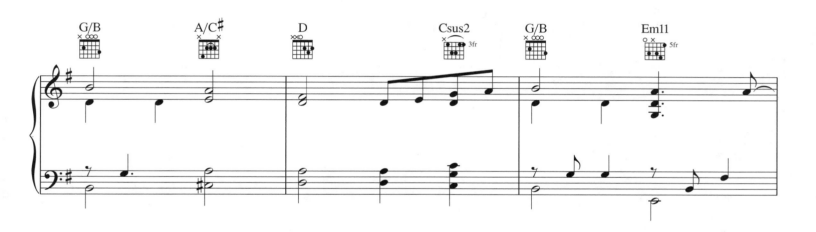

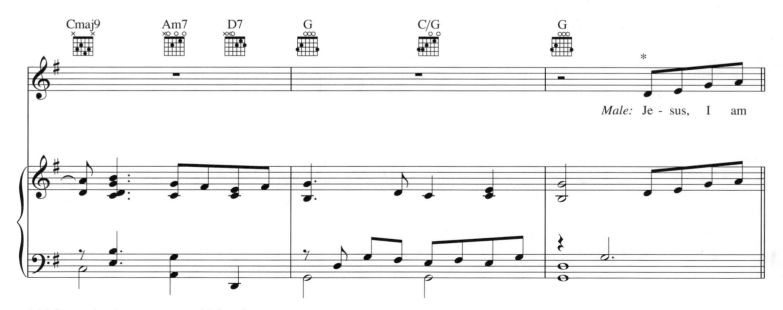

Male: Je - sus, I am

* *Male vocal written one octave higher than sung.*

rest - ing, rest - ing _____ in the joy of

what Thou art. _____ I am find - ing

out _____ the _____ great - ness of Thy lov - ing heart. _

IN CHRIST ALONE

Words and Music by DON KOCH
and SHAWN CRAIG

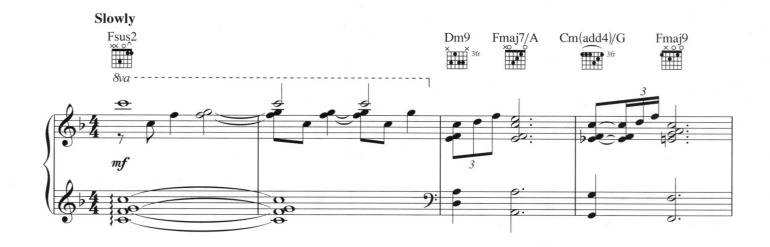

Female: In Christ a-lone____ will I glo-ry,____ though

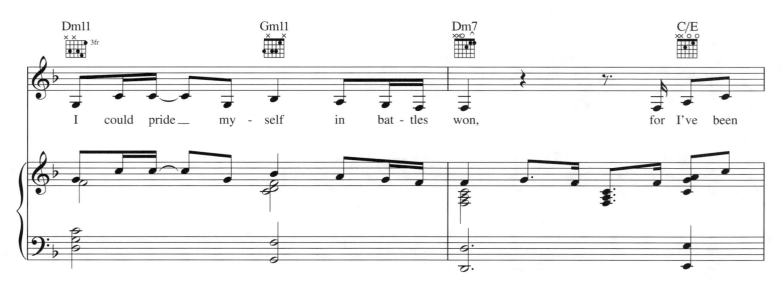

I could pride____ my-self in bat-tles won, for I've been

* Male vocal written one octave higher than sung.

GENTLE SHEPHERD/LEANING ON THE EVERLASTING ARMS

GENTLE SHEPHERD
Words by GLORIA GAITHER
Music by WILLIAM J. GAITHER

LEANING ON THE EVERLASTING ARMS
Traditional
Arranged by BILL BAUMGART

* Male vocal sung as written throughout a cappella section.

Male vocal written one octave higher than sung.

LORD MOST HIGH

Words and Music by DON HARRIS
and GARY SADLER

Moderately slow, in 2

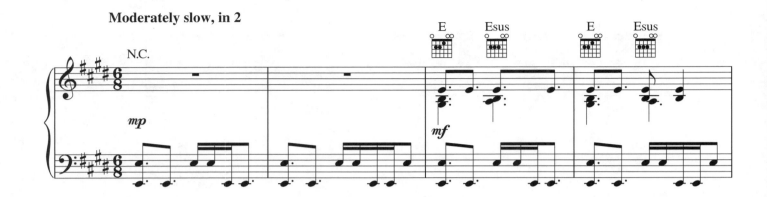

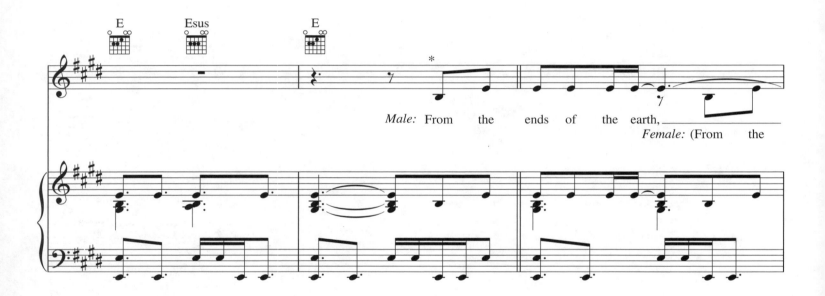

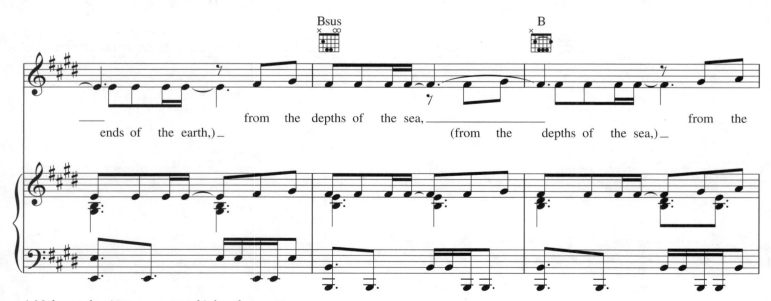

* Male vocal written one octave higher than sung.

raise, Lord. Through-out the end-less a-ges

You will be crowned with prais-es, Lord most

high. _____ Ex-alt-ed in ev-'ry na-tion,

sov-'reign of all cre-a-tion, Lord most

MY JESUS, I LOVE THEE

Words by WILLIAM R. FEATHERSTONE
Music by ADONIRAM J. GORDON
Arranged by THE MARTINS
and ROBERT WHITE JOHNSON

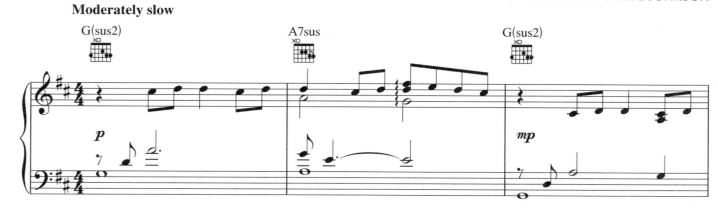

Original key: D♭ major. This edition has been transposed up one half-step to be more playable.

* Male vocal written one octave higher than sung.